"It's Unlucky to Be Behind at the End of the Game"
and Other Great Sports Retorts

"It's Unlucky to Be Behind at the End of the Game"
and Other Great Sports Retorts

DICK CROUSER

Illustrated by Jeff Danziger

QUILL
New York · 1983

Library of Congress Cataloging in Publication Data

Crouser, R. L.
"It's unlucky to be behind at the end of the game"
and other great sports retorts.

1. Sports—Anecdotes, facetiae, satire, etc.
I. Danziger, Jeff.   II. Title.
[GV707.C76   1983b]   796'.0207   82-23094
ISBN 0-688-01968-4
ISBN 0-688-01970-6 (pbk.)

Printed in the United States of America

First Quill Edition

1 2 3 4 5 6 7 8 9 10

BOOK DESIGN BY LINEY LI

Introduction

As a lifelong, incurable sports fan, I can't imagine a more pleasant task than the one I took on in putting together this collection. Think of it: a legitimate excuse to indulge myself in literally thousands of newspapers, magazines and books in search of the great "sports retort"!

I was looking for humorous sports situations that could be described briefly, that were true, and in which the punch line was a quote. Along the way, I've tried to eliminate most of those that seemed too familiar (or too phony) and to keep the truly funny. But then, truly funny is for *you* to decide.

So let's push on. On to some of what Casey Stengel must have had in mind when he said, "That's what makes sports the wonderful game it is."

C asey Stengel's eye for talent was often as keen as his wit. Early in his managerial career with the New York Mets, he was asked about the future prospects for two of his twenty-year-old players. "In ten years, Ed Kranepool has a chance to be a star," said Casey. "In ten years the other guy has a chance to be thirty."

I f you ever noticed football coach Frank Broyles look away from the field when his team was in a third-and-long situation, it was not just that he was nervous. It's simply that he was avoiding any eye contact with his quarterback. "I tell the quarterback never to look to me for a play in that situation," says Broyles. "After all, he's on a four-year scholarship and I'm sittin' here with a one-year contract."

G reater love hath no man for the game of handball than Minnesota's Wayne Stewart hath. Stewart, nationally ranked at various times, was playing a Sunday pickup game and suddenly, to his shock and dismay, realized he'd lost to a mere local club player. He demanded a rematch, and the first mutually agreeable time was 2 P.M. the following Saturday. But then, emerging from the shower, Stewart said, "Wait a minute. I just remembered that at two o'clock Saturday my daughter's getting married." "Well, does that mean you can't make it?" asked the other guy. Stewart agonized for several long moments, and then, "Boy, I don't know," he said, "my wife'd be madder'n hell."

J immy Piersall was just as controversial as a baseball player as he became later as an announcer. He was in and out of psychiatric treatment several times during his checkered career, but later decided that that was a special advantage. "I was supposed to throw things and keep nothing bottled up," said Piersall. "The same things used to cost Ted Williams five hundred dollars."

O kay, so rules are rules. And nobody's stickier about it than Harold Haydon was. Haydon was the dean of students at the University of Chicago when that school was challenged to an international tiddledywinks match by England's Cambridge College. As Chicago eagerly accepted, Dean Haydon sternly cautioned that "only students who maintain the university's academic standards will be eligible."

T here were a number of theories on why Oklahoma football star Joe Don Looney didn't stick around the NFL very long. The controversial Looney had tremendous talent—a talent matched only by his intense dislike for conformity and authority. He declined to take orders from coaches, assistant coaches, general managers, and owners alike. He wouldn't even throw his dirty towels into the right bin. "No stupid sign is gonna tell *me* what to do," said Looney.

I t was said of baseball immortal Rogers Hornsby that he had an infallible eye, that he *never* went for a bad pitch. One day, with Hornsby at bat, a rookie pitcher complained bitterly about three straight called balls. Then, at 3-0, he grooved one and Hornsby hit it about eight miles. As the great man circled the bases, plate umpire Bill Klem strolled to the mound and said, "Young man, you must never question a call when Mr. Hornsby is at bat. When the ball is over the plate, Mr. Hornsby will let you know."

T hey were at the sixteenth hole at Firestone in Akron, Ohio, and Sam Snead consulted his caddie on club selection for his approach shot. "Jay Hebert hit an eight-iron from right here yesterday," said the caddie. Snead pulled out an 8-iron and hit the shot right into the lake fronting the green. "Where did Hebert *hit* his eight-iron yesterday?" asked Snead. "Into the lake," said the caddie.

✳

T alk about talking yourself out of a job! A free agent placekicker wasn't doing too well during a tryout with John McKay's Tampa Bay Buccaneers. "I get nervous kicking in front of Coach McKay," he told reporters. "I don't think he's got much of a future here," said McKay. "I plan on being at most of the games."

✳

O ne of the requirements for being a successful athlete is having absolute confidence in your own abilities. So, did tennis pro Vitas Gerulaitis think it unusual when he defeated Jimmy Connors after having lost sixteen matches in a row to Connors? Apparently not. "*Nobody* beats me seventeen straight," said Gerulaitis.

G olf great Walter Hagen was known for his great skill, his ample capacity for liquid spirits, and his boundless self-confidence. He once bet ten dollars he would make a hole in one on the next hole . . . and did it! Reminded that that happens about once every 100,000 tee shots, the Haig explained, "The trick is to know when that one time is about to happen."

*

B ob Cousy, taking the short inbounds pass after the opposition had scored, wheeled and arched a long pass the length of the court, trying to work the fast break. He missed his man by quite a bit. In fact, the ball went right through the far hoop for a basket. Audience and players alike were stunned. Not Cousy. As he walked by the nearest opposing player, still frozen in his tracks, Cousy said, "You guys don't play much defense, do you?"

*

W hen rowing enthusiasts at Clemson came to athletic director Frank Howard for financial aid, they got short shrift. "Clemson will never subsidize a sport where a man sits on his tail and goes backwards," said Howard.

I n his day, freewheeling quarterback Bobby Layne was known to break training now and then. Layne's former teammate, Jimmy Orr, gives us an example. "You'll run into a million fans who'll claim they once had a drink with Bobby Layne somewhere," says Orr. "And none of them are lying."

✳

S ince ex-Yankee Jim Bouton turned author, he hasn't been above exploiting the foibles of some of his former playmates. On Billy Martin: "Lots of people look up to Billy," says Bouton. "That's because he's just knocked them down."

✳

I t helps for a linebacker to be packing a bit of heft, but how about a goalie? Minnesota North Star goalie Don Beaupre, all of 5 feet 8 inches and 149 pounds, doesn't think so. "I just have to stop the puck," says Beaupre, "not beat it to death."

O ne of the hazards of going to a racetrack is the ever-present horde of pickpockets. But according to a man who works there, New York's Belmont Park is the worst track of all. "When we had a skydiving exhibition here recently," he noted, "one parachutist felt a hand in his pocket before he even touched the ground."

✳

I t's as difficult to top Muhammad Ali verbally as it used to be to beat him in the ring. But a stewardess on an Eastern Airlines flight squelched him quite nicely when the Great Man balked at fastening his seat belt.

Ali: "Superman don't need no seat belt."

Stewardess: "Superman don't need no airplane, either."

✳

J ust how powerful *was* Twins slugger Harmon Killebrew? Plenty, according to veteran baseball man Paul Richards. "Killebrew could hit the ball out of any park in the country," says Richards. "And that includes Yellowstone."

U mpires take a lot of grief from fans and players alike. It just sort of comes with the territory. But once in a while one of them gets a chance to strike back. Yankee pitcher Bob Turley was having a tough day and he was taking it out on umpire Ed Hurley. Finally, Turley came off the mound to complain bitterly about a call. And he got a bit personal. But Hurley just smiled. "Say whatever you like, I'm not gonna throw you out," said Hurley. "I'm gonna let them *knock* you out."

W hen Bowden Wyatt coached football at Tennessee, he didn't put a whole lot of stress on stunts or fancy routes for his defensive backs. His idea of pursuit was clear and simple. "Take the shortest possible route to the ball carrier," he said, "and arrive in a bad humor."

G rady Alderman's main job with the early Vikings was to supply pass protection for his ever-scrambling quarterback, Fran Tarkenton. And he really knew his man. Once, when a fallen defensive end tried to get up too quickly, Grady fell on the man and pinned him. Referring to the departed Tarkenton, the irritated defender said, "*Okay*, let me up . . . he's gone!" "He's gone," said Grady, "but he'll probably be back."

I n New York one night back in the 1960s, light heavyweight Willie Pastrano was having a problem. His companion in the ring, Jose Torres, had dropped him several times in the early rounds and now, in the fifth, decked him again. As Willie just beat the count, the ring doctor rushed in to check his condition. "Are you okay, Willie? Do you know where you are?" he asked. "You're damn right I do," said Pastrano. "I'm in Madison Square Garden gettin' the hell kicked outa me!"

✳

R eggie Jackson is a pretty smart guy, but some of his teammates haven't always appreciated hearing about it from Reggie himself. "My IQ is 160," he once told Mickey Rivers. "Out of what," said Rivers, "a thousand?"

✳

A few years back, some Cincinnati Bengal fans suspected that the rise of the intellectual football player had contributed to the club's decline in the standings. "The Bengals need some players," said one, "who speak only in one-syllable words, eat bananas, and have to be chained to the bench."

W hen a pro athlete is married and travels a lot, he needs a wife who is considerate, sympathetic, and understanding. "My wife doesn't care what I do when I'm away," says golfer Lee Trevino, "as long as I don't have a good time."

✳

I n all of pro football history, there have been few pass catchers as glue-fingered as former Colt great Raymond Berry. During the 1979 season, New England Patriot head coach Ron Erhardt was asked why his receivers, tutored by Raymond Berry, now an assistant coach, were dropping so many passes. "Simple," said Erhardt, "Raymond is coachin' 'em, not catchin' 'em."

✳

I t was umpire Marty Springstead's first major league game and the formidable 250-pound Frank Howard was at bat. Springstead called the first pitch, at the knees, a strike. "Get something straight, buster," growled Howard. "On me that pitch is never a strike!" Next pitch, same place. "Two!" said Springstead. "Two what!" roared Howard. "Too low, Frank," said Springstead. "Much too low."

F amous golf club thrower Tommy Bolt was nearing the end of a frustrating round, during which his temper had shown through a few times. Looking over a shot of about 150 yards to the green, he asked his caddie which club he should use. "I'd say either a five-iron or a wedge," said the caddie. "A five-iron or a wedge! What kind of a choice is *that*?" asked Bolt. "Those are the only two clubs you have left, sir," said the caddie.

B asketball great Bill Russell wasn't always the avid golfer he became in later years. "When I was growing up, my mother wouldn't allow me near a golf course," says Russell. "She didn't think golfers were very nice people. Now that I play every day, I realize that she was right."

✳

F irst baseman Marv Throneberry had many thrilling adventures during the early days of the hapless New York Mets. Marvelous Marv once hit a booming triple, only to be called out when the opposition claimed he had missed second base. As manager Casey Stengel charged out to protest the call, he was stopped by the first base coach. "Don't bother, Casey," said the coach, "he didn't touch first base, either."

✳

G olf immortal Ben Hogan was sometimes called the Iceman, in recognition of his coolness under pressure *and* of his not being overly chatty on the course. But Jimmy Demaret was quick to come to Ben's defense. "I can't understand why people say Ben is so untalkative," said Demaret. "He speaks to me on every green. He says, 'You're away.'"

Major league baseball talent was probably never spread quite so thin as it was in 1945, with hundreds of regulars off fighting World War II. That year, as the patchwork Cubs and Tigers limped home to pennants in their respective leagues, questions arose about which would take the World Series. "I don't think either of them can win it," said sportswriter Warren Brown.

✳

The world's record for fewest words spoken during a round of golf is zero, and is held by several tight-lipped notables. All alone in second place, with one word, is the immortal Harry Vardon. Vardon was playing a not very sociable round with Bobby Jones when, late in the match, Jones hit one of his rare bad shots. "Did you ever *see* a worse shot than that!" fumed Jones. "No," said Vardon.

✳

A couple of priests at Creighton University, both avid basketball fans, were listening intently to a delayed radio broadcast of the school's narrow win over Bradley. As the lead changed back and forth, one of them said, "Why am I so nervous? I *know* how this turns out!" "Now you know how God must feel," said the other.

I f you sometimes resent paying full price to see an NFL preseason game only to watch many of the star players ride the bench, you have a champion in sportswriter Glenn Sheeley. On his coverage of exhibition games, Sheeley says, "If the coaches don't play a lot of their starters, I don't use any of my first-string verbs and adjectives."

❋

O utfielder Jackie Brandt hung on, with his barely acceptable .262 lifetime batting average, for eleven years with four different big league teams. But it wasn't easy. At the end of one season with Baltimore, Brandt was cleaning out his locker when Oriole president Lee Mac-Phail walked by. "Have a good winter, Jackie," said MacPhail. "I always have good winters," said Brandt. "It's the summers that give me trouble."

❋

S ometimes there are indirect factors that influence a manager's decision to remove a pitcher from a game. Texas Ranger Jim Kern once disagreed with the manager's suggestion that he take an early shower. "I told him I wasn't tired," Kern said, "and he said, 'No, but the outfielders sure are.'"

O ne of the agonies of being a football coach is the long post mortem after a loss. North Carolina's Jim Tatum once described how he lies in bed the night after a loss tossing and turning and wondering why he ordered a kick here, a pass there, and a run the other time. Is it a lonely feeling? "No," said Tatum. "I know that all over the state there are thousands of other folks wondering the same things."

✳

F ormer Dallas Cowboy Pete Gent gives us some insights on Coach Tom Landry's approach to the game when he recalls advising a rookie about Landry's playbook. "Don't read it, kid," said Gent. "Everybody gets killed in the end."

✳

L egendary golfer Walter Hagen never let false modesty get in the way of the truth. As midnight came and went on the eve of a big PGA title match, the Haig showed little sign of deserting the host club's bar. The concerned bartender finally reminded him that his opponent had been in bed for hours. Hagen's reply was reassuring. "Young man," he said, "he may have retired, but he knows who he's playing tomorrow and you may be sure he hasn't slept a wink."

Branch Rickey was the Brooklyn general manager when Bobby Bragan managed the Dodger farm club in Fort Worth. In an economy move Rickey once decreed that there be no more long-distance phone calls between headquarters and the farm teams—letters or telegrams would do. Soon after, Rickey wired Bragan: DO YOU NEED A SHORTSTOP OR IS PRESENT INFIELD OKAY?

Bragan wired Rickey: YES.

Rickey wired Bragan: YES WHAT?

Bragan wired Rickey: YES, SIR!

England's yacht *Sceptre* had just been thrashed soundly in the 1959 America's Cup Races and syndicate chairman Hugh Goodson was discussing his group's stiff-upper-lip plans for another all-Britain effort, scheduled three years hence. Was there any reason to believe that the results would be any different in 1962? "There is considerable optimism," said Goodson, "among two or three people."

C onsidering how many years comedian Bob Hope has played golf, one would think that by now he'd have mastered all phases of the game. Not so, according to pro golfer Jimmy Demaret. "Bob has a beautiful short game," says Demaret. "Unfortunately, it's off the tee."

✳

I n 1978 Gaylord Perry was being interviewed after a win that, once again, relief ace Rollie Fingers had saved for him. Noting that a 300-win career total seemed quite possible for Perry, a reporter asked if he might aim for Cy Young's all-time record of 511 victories. "I'll never make that," said Perry. "Rollie won't live that long."

✳

J ohnny Mize was better known for his work with the bat than with the glove. While with the Giants, his feeble efforts around first base prompted humorist Goodman Ace to wire Giant manager Leo Durocher, SIR, BEFORE EACH GAME AN ANNOUNCEMENT IS MADE THAT ANYONE INTERFERING WITH OR TOUCHING A BATTED BALL WILL BE EJECTED FROM THE PARK. PLEASE INFORM MR. MIZE THAT THIS DOES NOT REFER TO HIM.

I t seems that there are fringe benefits to being President. After leaving the White House, Dwight Eisenhower was asked if he noticed anything different about his golf game. "Yes," he said, "a lot more people beat me now."

O ld-time second baseman Billy Herman had no doubts about who was the greatest brushback pitcher of all time. "It's gotta be Freddy Fitzsimmons," said Herman. "He once hit me in the on-deck circle."

T hings were especially bleak for the New Hampshire basketball teams in the early 1960s. Once, when Davidson crushed them 115–54, a New Hampshire fan supplied this explanation, "Our biggest trouble is that we had a real poor season last year and most of our regulars returned."

W e all know that baseball fights usually don't amount to much. But what about hockey brawls—are they for real? When Rod Gilbert was with the New York Rangers, he assured the world that hockey fights are definitely in earnest. "If they were fake," he said, "you'd see me *in* more of them."

W hen Bucky Harris managed the old Washington Senators, his teams were never noted for their batting ability. But at least he was realistic about it. One day, with the Senators facing Cleveland's fireballing Bob Feller, Bucky gave his team some practical advice. "Go up and hit what you see," he said. "And if you don't see anything, come on back."

*

T he 1946 Army-Notre Dame game was one of college football's classics. And the defensive highlight of the match was Army's Arnold Tucker's three interceptions of Johnny Lujack's passes. When Fighting Irish coach Frank Leahy asked the usually accurate Lujack about it, Johnny had a ready reply. "Tucker was the only man open," he said.

*

S ometimes, even though they're only a few feet apart, a boxer and his corner men have a different perspective on how a fight is going. Coming to his corner at the end of a round midway through his title bout with Joe Louis, Max Baer heard one of his seconds say, "Good goin', Max, he ain't laid a glove on you." "Well then you'd better watch that referee," said Baer, "'cause somebody's beatin' the hell outa me."

When Cesar Cedeno was traded from the Houston Astros to Cincinnati, he was immensely relieved that the Reds let him keep his Houston uniform number, 28. Superstitious? "No," said Cedeno, "I've just got too much jewelry with number twenty-eight on it."

✳

"Running to daylight" was Vince Lombardi's way of describing a good ball carrier. Now Bum Phillips has altered the phrase to compare two of the better running backs he's worked with. "George Rogers *sees* daylight," says Phillips. "Earl Campbell *makes* daylight."

✳

Ralph Kiner has seen plenty of outfielding in his time, but he's obviously impressed with both the fielding skills and the range of fleet center fielder Garry Maddox. "The earth is two-thirds covered by water," says Kiner. "The other third is covered by Garry Maddox."

After averaging a healthy 45 yards on eleven kicks in a game with Houston, Buffalo punter Paul Maguire was asked to comment on kicking conditions at the Astrodome. "I think that both the placekicker and I got a little more distance in the second and fourth quarters when we had the air conditioning at our backs," he said.

TURN UP
THE
AIR-CONDITIONING!!

T he Dallas Mavericks weren't going to give away *anything* to the Utah Jazz and big Adrian Dantley that night. When assistant coach Bob Weiss was asked how many points the Mavericks would allow Dantley to get, he replied, "We're not going to allow him *any*, but he'll probably get a bunch anyway."

✳

W hen Pete Elliot coached football at the University of Miami, he had to give one young high school prospect high marks for honesty. "I asked him if he was in the top half of his class academically," said Elliot. "He said, 'No, sir. I'm one of those who make the top half possible.'"

✳

I n 1931 good-field-no-hit Fresco Thompson was traded to the Dodgers and found himself with a locker next to that of good hitter, bad fielder Babe Herman. "Damn," said slugger Herman, scornfully. "They're makin' me dress next to a .250 hitter." "Damn," said Thompson. "They're makin' *me* dress next to a .250 *fielder*."

J ack Kemp went directly from one big league to another—from quarterbacking the NFL's Buffalo Bills to serving in the U.S. Congress as a representative from Buffalo. His election strategy? "I told the voters that if they didn't elect me," said Kemp, "I'd come back and play another year for the Bills."

✳

D on't ever knock the School of Hard Knocks. University of Washington defensive tackle Fletcher Jenkins had taken a summer job operating a jackhammer because he thought it would add to his upper-body strength. Did it work? "What it did was tear my arms apart and teach me the value of a college education," said Jenkins.

✳

U niversity of Oklahoma basketball coach Billy Tubbs believes in taking things one step at a time. When asked how his fast break offense would do in the season just ahead, he put the matter into perspective. "This year we plan to run and shoot," said Tubbs. "Next season we hope to run and score."

T he "country club" label attached to the Boston Red Sox for so long had more to do with playing around than with playing golf (or, for that matter, baseball). In his day, pitcher Gene Conley was one of the foremost revelers, and his passion and capacity for beer were legendary. He once returned to the clubhouse after a two-day absence and explained to Manager Mike Higgins that there had been an illness in the family. "Who was sick?" asked Higgins. "Me," said Conley.

A thletes are probably the most superstitious of all the earth's creatures. Some won't step on the foul line or the sideline, others won't shave during a winning streak, and on and on. When he was coaching at Michigan State, Duffy Daugherty had only one hang-up. "My only feeling about superstition," said Duffy, "is that it's unlucky to be behind at the end of the game."

T here was never any doubt about what Don Cherry wanted to be when *he* grew up. "When I said my prayers as a kid I'd always tell the Lord I wanted to be a pro hockey player," says Cherry. "Unfortunately, I forgot to mention the NHL, so I spent sixteen years in the minors."

Do hockey goalies sometimes feel that they're operating in a fishbowl? Subjected to too much harsh criticism? Well, Hall of Famer Jacques Plante sounds a bit defensive, but here's the comparison he makes. "How'd you like it if you were sitting in your office and you made one tiny little mistake," says Plante, "and eighteen thousand people jump up and start shouting obscenities at you?"

Ask any major league umpire to list his favorite people and manager Earl Weaver will probably not be anywhere near the top. To say that Mr. Weaver is vocal in his periodic objections to official decisions would be something of an understatement. Umpire Marty Springstead puts it this way. "The best way to test a Timex watch," says Springstead, "would be to tie it to Earl Weaver's tongue."

Football coach Lou Holtz likes to look on the bright side of things. When his Arkansas team was tuning up for an Orange Bowl game, he was warned that his squad might be the target of orange-tossing fans there. "Could be worse," said Holtz. "We could be going to the Gator Bowl."

A football coach has to keep coming up with new and different ways to inspire his team just before the "big game." John Madden tells about his speech to the Oakland Raiders in the final minutes before Super Bowl XI. "I told 'em, 'Don't worry about the horse bein' blind, just load the wagon.'" What does *that* mean? "I don't have the slightest idea," said Madden.

If clothes make the man, maybe it follows that uniforms make the athlete. At least Groucho Marx seemed to think so. Groucho was dining in New York one night when Joe DiMaggio walked into the restaurant. And it upset him to see the Yankee Clipper idling about in civilian clothes. "Suppose a game broke out in the middle of the night," Groucho protested. "By the time he got suited up, it might be all over."

The pressures of quarterbacking a major college or pro football team can be pretty intense. But when Dan Marino played that position at Pitt, his truck driver father wasn't all that impressed. "Don't tell me about pressure," said the elder Marino. "Pressure is having five kids and a mortgage and just getting laid off from your job."

During their first few years the New York Mets were such a study in futility that a player had to do something especially bad even to be noticed. Such as the brand-new relief pitcher's performance when he entered his first game with the score tied in the bottom of the twelfth. He stretched and threw and had his very first pitch slammed for a game-winning home run. "He makes the team," said a perceptive teammate.

✳

Golfer Lee Trevino is as much fun to listen to as he is to watch. One plentiful source of his stories is his less than affluent childhood. How poor were the Trevinos? "We had so little to eat," says Lee, "that when Mom would throw a bone to the dog, he'd have to call for a fair catch."

✳

Among the usual reasons most people give for favoring such organized youth activities as Little League baseball is that it "keeps the kids off the streets." However, Yogi Berra—as he does on most topics—has his own way of putting things. Little League? "Keeps the kids outa the house," says Yogi.

When 320-pound tackle Angelo Fields first reported to the Houston Oilers, someone asked coach Bum Phillips if he thought the rookie should trim down to 300 pounds or so. "Heck no," said Phillips, "the kid's *bones* weigh three hundred pounds."

✳

When the late Al Helfer was broadcasting the Oakland A's games, he was not too enthusiastic about Reggie Jackson's speed. Or his hustle. Once, with Jackson on third, teammate Rick Monday hit a long home run. "Jackson should score easily on that one," commented Helfer.

✳

When the young New York Mets were struggling to gain some respectability, Mets Board Chairman M. Donald Grant urged their fans to have patience. "After all," he explained, "you don't breed a thoroughbred horse overnight." Which left some of the fans hoping Grant knew more about baseball than he did about breeding horses.

W hen coach Bob Devaney was riding high at Nebraska, he was asked why he didn't ask for a lifetime contract. His reasoning: "I once had a friend with a lifetime contract. Then, after two bad years in a row, the president called him into his office and declared him dead."

C harlie Waters of the Dallas Cowboys was impressed. He was watching a computerized game that pitted the 1971 Cowboys against a team that included, among other all-time greats, the immortal Jim Thorpe. "For an eighty-four-year-old Indian," said Waters, "he showed me some great moves."

✳

S lugger Dick Stuart's shortcomings in the field earned him the nickname Dr. Strangeglove. But if Stuart was a bit inept at fielding his position, he showed a touch of class in other ways. Joining Pittsburgh midway through the 1958 season, his hot bat helped the Pirates to a respectable place in the final standings. He was then voted a mere half-share of the year-end bonus money—the same amount awarded the team's batboy. "But you must understand," said Stuart, "he's a *very* good batboy."

✳

I n spite of America's roads and paths being choked with joggers, the pastime does have its detractors. Former University of Texas basketball coach Abe Lemons spoke for all of them when, asked if he were a jogger, he said, "Hell, no. When I die I want to be sick."

D ick "Kayo" Tobin was one of those "semipro" athletes who talks a good game—no matter what the game. In the realm of boxing he once claimed an unusual record. Tobin claimed that, as a boxer, he once had 127 pro fights without losing a decision. "I got knocked out every time," said Tobin. Then, for good measure, he adds, "The last guy I fought hit me with thirty-seven lucky right hands."

✳

B ack when $20,000 was a fabulous salary for a major league star, Yankee pitching ace Lefty Gomez got quite a shock. After a so-so year, Gomez was asked to take a pay cut from $20,000 all the way down to $7,500. "Tell you what," said Gomez to the Yankee owner, "you keep the salary and pay me the cut."

✳

T he Southwest Louisiana basketball team (the Ragin' Cajuns) was being badly thumped by Pan American. But when the Cajuns scored to narrow the margin to 93–77, they called a time-out. With just one second remaining on the clock. "Oh, oh," said Cajun radio announcer Don Allen, "here comes that sixteen-point play we've been working on."

A s any hitter from his era could confirm, pitcher Sal Maglie was not called the Barber for any skills with a razor or shears. It was, rather, for the many close shaves he administered with his famous knockdown pitches. In fact, Maglie always recommended throwing not one but *two* brushbacks. "The second one," he explained, "lets the hitter know you meant the first one."

What do you say when you're just a St. Louis Cardinal rookie, you're out after curfew, and sneaking back into the hotel, you run smack into the team president? Pitcher Dizzy Dean's solution was simple. "You and me could catch hell for this Mr. Ankenman," said Diz, "but I won't say nuthin' if you don't."

✳

Year after year, there are few college football teams as consistently tough as the Cornhuskers of Nebraska. But coach Donnie Duncan, whose Iowa State team had just been stomped by them, was able to see the bright side. "There are lots of teams better than Nebraska," said Duncan. "Fortunately, most of them are in the NFL."

✳

At least former Yankee pitching great Lefty Gomez knew *somebody* liked him. He was locked in a salary dispute with Yankee owner Colonel Ruppert. Lefty wanted more money, but the Colonel wouldn't budge. "Then some of the hitters around the league got together," says Lefty, "and offered to chip in to pay me the difference."

At last! The answer to all a duffer's problems has become simple: Buy your own golf course. When asked what par was for the course he had just bought, singer Willie Nelson said, "Anything I want it to be. This hole right here, for instance, is a par forty-seven . . . and yesterday I birdied the sucker!"

＊

When pitching great Dizzy Dean switched from the mound to the broadcasting booth, he drew howls of protest from teachers and parents for some liberties he took with the language: "The runner slud into second," for example. How important *is* good grammar? "Lotsa people who don't say ain't," said Dean, "ain't eatin'."

＊

The Browns and the Steelers were tied and, with just 9 seconds left in the overtime period, Pittsburgh's Matt Bahr came in to try for the game-winning field goal. What do you say to your placekicker to ease the tension at a time like that? "I tried not to put any pressure on him," said Steeler quarterback Terry Bradshaw. "I said, 'Miss it and you're cut.'"

At one time pro golfer Billy Casper was as well known for his exotic diet as he was for his prowess on the links. But according to one sportswriter, there were those who questioned the impact that the Casper menu actually had on his game. For example, Billy's buffalo meat and other special rations were late in arriving at a tournament and, after a first-round 75, he complained that some coffee shop sausage had upset his stomach. Overhearing this, his partner, Miller Barber, turned to a friend and said, "Bad sausage and five bogeys'll give a guy a stomachache every time."

Does it get boring for the pro golfer to play every hole in regulation: drive down the middle of the fairway, hit the green, and then two-putt? Why not take a few chances and get some thrills? Lee Trevino tells us why not. "There are two things not long for this world," he says, "dogs who chase cars and pro golfers who chip for pars."

The basketball game between Wisconsin and Northwestern was a big one . . . the two were tied for last place in the Big Ten. Then, as Wisconsin pulled it out in the last few seconds, happy Badger fans started chanting, "We're number nine!"

F ew teams in baseball history have been as inept as the wartime St. Louis Browns of 1945. After his Indians had thrashed the Browns in a late-season game, Cleveland manager Lou Boudreau, consoling rival skipper Luke Sewell, said, "You know, Luke, we just *may* have figured out some of your signals." "Would you mind explaining them to *my* team?" said Sewell. "They haven't learned them yet."

✳

C omedian-golfer Jackie Gleason has many of the problems that most of us have hitting decent tee shots. But when his waistline got out of control he had an extra, "built-in" handicap. "When I tee the ball where I can see it, I can't hit it," said Gleason. "And when I put it where I can hit it, I can't see it."

✳

T rue superstars are hard to come by. A truly *modest* superstar is even more rare. But pro football's Earl Campbell seems to qualify. He so consistently credits his teammates for his own success that one Houston newsman has said, "If it were up to Earl, he'd change the name of the 'I' formation to the 'We.'"

When Norm Van Brocklin quarterbacked the Philadelphia Eagles, their offensive line was so porous one year that Van Brocklin suffered an unusually high number of indignities. When asked about the frequency with which he'd been forced to eat the ball, he said, "If the ball had had calories, I'd have weighed three thousand pounds by the end of the year."

O nce, during a pro-amateur event, golfer Dutch Harrison had a particularly annoying amateur partner. The man would press Dutch for advice on almost every shot, and then usually botch it. Late in the round the duffer found his errant drive sitting in the middle of a bush. "How shall I play it, Dutch?" he asked. "Under an assumed name," said Harrison.

✳

W hen the 1979–80 Boston Celtics got off to a much better start than they had the year before, center Dave Cowens gave all the credit to the coaching. "Last year's coach didn't have the experience, the know-how, or the intelligence," said Cowens. Last year's coach: Dave Cowens.

✳

D uring his last year as a player, with Durocher's New York Giants, Joe Garagiola was having his usual problems at the plate. In one crucial game, he came up with the bases loaded . . . and fanned. He vowed to redeem himself and, next time up, he got his chance. Again the bases were full of Giants, and this time Garagiola smashed one . . . right into a double play. Durocher was furious. "C'mon, Garagiola, be a *team* player!" he screamed. "Strike out!"

Pro golfer Miller Barber was having his problems in a big fairway trap at England's Lytham course. His ball was deeply imbedded and he was being carefully watched by a rather critical British gallery. He blasted once and the ball barely moved. Another mighty swing produced only a big spray of sand. At this point a very proper lady observer was heard to remark, "Fancy coming all the way from America to do *that*."

Ex-boxer Archie Moore does a lot of public speaking, and much of it is within prison walls talking with convicts. What does he like best about his sessions? "Nobody can walk out on my speech," said Archie.

Part of being a successful coach is really understanding your players. Florida State football coach Bobby Bowden seemed to have star linebacker Reggie Herring pretty well figured. "He doesn't know the meaning of the word fear," said Bowden. "In fact, I just saw his grades and he doesn't know the meaning of a lot of words."

W hen George Brett was making a serious run at hitting .400 during the 1980 season, nobody was pulling harder for him to succeed than the last man to do it, Ted Williams. How come? "Then people would stop asking me if I thought anyone else could ever do it," said Williams. "They could ask him."

※

T he jet age has made it much easier for an athlete to widen his or her sphere—to compete all over the globe. But it's been a mixed blessing to those who fear flying. One of these, British boxer Terry Downes, once explained why he continued to make his transatlantic hops by boat. "I can swim a bit," said Downes, "but I can't fly at all."

※

W hen Cardinals pitcher Bob Gibson was at his peak, his many skills were obvious to all. That's why it came as quite a surprise to those who heard Gibson's former catcher, Tim McCarver, describe Gibson as a *lucky* pitcher. "Lucky?" asked one. "Sure," said McCarver. "He always seems to pitch on the day the other team doesn't score any runs."

T he bus driver had misjudged the time it would take him to get the Minnesota Vikings from their hotel to the stadium to play the Detroit Lions. Now, bogged down in heavy pregame traffic as kickoff time neared, he waved frantically to a nearby policeman for help. "I have to get to the game!" shouted the driver. "I've got the Vikings!" "Big deal!" yelled the cop. "I've got the Lions and six!"

✳

W restler Bull Montana never actually excelled at his chosen profession. And later, as a wrestler-turned-actor, he was also something short of sensational. But for pure, unadulterated ugliness, Montana was in a class by himself. How ugly was he? "Bull Montana is so ugly," said one admirer, "that he can make up for the role of a chimpanzee simply by removing his hat."

✳

W hen George Bamberger was managing the Milwaukee Brewers, he was asked to comment on the triple play that his team had been a victim of the day before. "It pretty much took us right out of the inning," he observed.

Even Jose Cruz will admit that he's not as good with a glove as he is with a bat in his hands. But he can't be as bad in the field as a teammate suggested when, early one season, Cruz came down with the chicken pox. "Maybe Jose catching the chicken pox is a good sign," said the player. "Last year he didn't catch anything."

D ick "Kayo" Tobin was the pretty-fair-all-around-amateur-athlete–real-life-policeman and humorist who used to show up to "try out" at the Baltimore Orioles spring training camp each year. Someone once asked him if he'd ever tried his hand at pro boxing. "Are you kidding?" said Tobin. "I once had Joe Louis down on one knee. He bent over to see if I was all right."

*

W hen coach John Mackovic's Wake Forest football team squeezed out a 22–21 victory over Georgia, it was considered a real upset. Asked if it was the biggest win of his coaching career, Mackovic allowed that, at the very worst, it had to rank right up there in his top three. Why? "I *have* only three wins so far," he said.

*

W hen Bobby Bonds went from the Indians to the St. Louis Cardinals it was his sixth team in six years. Apparently, the frequent change in scenery had its brighter side. "Hey," said Bonds, "I could be the first guy to play for all twenty-six teams."

I t's simply a matter of values—it's how you were "brung up." "Waste not, want not," and like that. Atlanta Falcons receiver Greg McCrary, who had played football for a small school in the South, was asked why he didn't go through a lot of end zone theatrics when he scored his first NFL touchdown. His answer: "One time in college I threw the ball up into the stands after a score . . . and they made me go up and get it."

✳

T he longest season had just ended with the hapless New York Mets chalking up their record 120th defeat. Manager Casey Stengel was, for once, at a loss for words as he struggled for a way to console the dejected squad. But not for long. "Don't be discouraged," Stengel said. "This has been a team effort. No one or two players could have done it by themselves."

✳

W hen the Reverend Dr. Felix Gear gained some prominence as the moderator of the Southern Presbyterian Church, he was interviewed on his life-style and hobbies. About his hunting prowess, he was quite frank. "I have hunted deer on occasion," said Gear, "but none of them ever became aware of it."

The legendary Dazzy Vance of the old Dodgers had a fastball that had the whole league talking . . . to themselves. The Cubs' Jigger Statz once complained bitterly to the ump about a called third strike Vance had thrown him. "Where was the pitch?" asked a teammate as Statz returned to the bench. "I don't know," said Jigger, "but it sounded low."

✳

One of the better stories about Vince Lombardi is undoubtedly just that—a story. But well worth hoping it really happened. It refers to the time when the Packers reigned supreme over all of football and Lombardi was omnipotent, the lord of all he surveyed. As he crawled wearily into bed late one night, the story goes, his wife stirred and complained, "God, your feet are cold!" "Here at home," said Lombardi, "you can call me Vince."

✳

It seems that John Bridgers, Florida State athletic director, changed his mind on what he had wanted most out of his coaching career: "When I was young I wanted to be the best coach in the nation," said Bridgers. "Later I just wanted to be the oldest."

I t was no fun hitting against Walter Johnson's incredible fastball even when the light was ideal. On a dark, overcast day, though, the experience could be terrifying. On one such day the Indians' Ray Chapman stepped reluctantly into the box and, after looking timidly at two blazing called strikes, headed back to the dugout. "You've got one more coming, Chapman," yelled the umpire. "Never mind," said Chapman. "I don't really want it."

✳

A sk almost anyone who is the all-time best promoter in baseball and the answer will invariably be either Charlie Finley or Bill Veeck. Ask Bill Veeck the same question and you won't get any "either-or" reply. Could that *possibly* mean that Veeck thinks Finley's promotions aren't original? "If I ever run out of ideas," says Veeck, "Finley is finished."

✳

S an Francisco 49ers coach Bill Walsh, explaining his team's losing their first seven games, said, "We have a young team. Many of them are in their first year." Then, after a moment's reflection, he added, "Of course, some of the same guys might be in their last year, too."

T he high cost of living (or playing) is getting to pro athletes, too. But with everything from golf balls to bowling balls continuing to go up in price, pro bowler Don Carter still thinks he's in the right sport. "You very seldom lose a bowling ball," says Carter.

✳

P layers' injuries are the curse of the coaching business . . . and a great topic for conversation. But L.A. Dodger manager Tom Lasorda has decided to avoid the subject. Why? "Eighty percent of the people who hear about your injuries don't care," said Lasorda, "and the other twenty percent are glad you're having trouble."

✳

E ven the greatest of golfers has his moments of frustration, just as you and I. But everything is relative. The usually placid Jack Nicklaus once stormed off the eighteenth green at the Tournament of Champions in Las Vegas after missing an eagle putt. "No matter how hard I try," fumed Nicklaus, "I just *can't* seem to break sixty-four." "That's a terrible thing to have to go through life with," sympathized a nearby writer.

A lot of old-time pro athletes used to pride themselves on their ability to "play hurt," to actually hide minor injuries for the sake of staying in the lineup. But self-preservation and the longer-range view are more the mark of today's athlete. As linebacker Reggie Williams put it, when asked to tick off his chief physical talents, "Speed, strength, and the ability to recognize pain immediately."

Does today's pro athlete have much control over his or her destiny? Here's Bob Asher's recollection of a phone conversation he had with Chicago Bears coach Abe Gibron minutes after Asher learned he'd been traded from Dallas to the Bears.

Gibron: "Bob, if you're not one hundred percent happy with coming to the Bears, just say so and I'll cancel the deal."

Asher: "Coach, there are a lot of places I don't want to play and Chicago is *all* of them."

Gibron: "Fine, Bob. We'll see you here on Tuesday."

As a hitter, nobody ever accused Danny O'Connell of being a major menace to pitchers. But he is in the record books, along with more than thirty others, for having once hit three triples in one game. Off Phillies ace Robin Roberts, no less. "Roberts and I talk about it every time I see him," says Danny. "I usually bring it up."

When Bob Aspromonte was playing third base for Houston, he fell into his worst slump ever. How bad is the worst? "I've heard of guys going oh for fifteen or oh for twenty-five," he said, "but I was oh for July."

After five years in the majors pitcher Pete Ramos finally struck out the great Ted Williams. So he saved the ball and, after the game, he asked Williams to autograph it. Next time they met in a game, Williams hit the first pitch completely out of sight. As he circled the bases, Thumpin' Ted yelled over at Ramos, "Go get that one and I'll sign it, too."

Tampa Bay football coach John McKay was not happy with his squad after a 42–14 drubbing at the hands of the underdog New Orleans Saints. In fact, he seemed to be suggesting that some of them had not put a whole lot of effort into their performance when he opened his postgame remarks with, "After you shower, if anybody thinks he really *needs* a shower . . ."

Charlie Dressen had few peers in the fine art of stealing other teams' signals. And he was, obviously, quite proud of his talent. During the pregame meeting when he managed the 1953 National League All-Stars, a player asked about the signs to be used. "Don't worry about it," said Charlie, "I'll give each of you the ones you use on your own team."

D uring a rare slump, it was revealed that golf titan Jack Nicklaus was working on reconstructing his swing. Fellow touring pro Don January was asked if he'd ever tried that. "The difference between me and Jack," said January, "is that I'm still trying to construct my *first* swing."

✳

N atural rivalries add a little something to any sporting event, no matter what anyone says to the contrary. Take it from former Houston coach Bum Phillips, jubilant after his Oilers had squeaked by the archenemy Dallas Cowboys. "I know I said that this was just another game," said Phillips, "but I lied."

✳

A Yankee official once told star pitcher Lefty Gomez that if he'd put on some weight he'd make the older fans forget about Jack Chesbro, who had once won 41 games for New York in a single season. Gomez added ten pounds over the winter and his record promptly plunged to 11-15. Had he made them forget Chesbro? "Hell," said Lefty, "I almost made 'em forget *Gomez*."

P aul Hornung, the former Notre Dame and Green Bay Packers great, was truly an all-around sport. On and off the field. When he finally married, he was asked why the ceremony was scheduled for 11 A.M., an early hour for the Golden Boy. "Because if it doesn't work out," said Hornung, "I don't want to blow the whole day."

✳

O ld-time outfielder Ping Bodie loved to steal bases, but his lack of speed was usually his undoing. Frustrated coaches and managers tried to dissuade him, but to no avail. Writer Bugs Baer summed it up when he said, of Bodie, "It's too bad . . . his head is full of larceny, but his feet are honest."

✳

O ne of Louisville basketball star Darrell Griffith's outstanding talents while at that school was his impressive jumping ability. One of those most impressed after playing against Griffith was Iowa's Bob Hansen. "I've guarded other guys who could leap high," said Hansen, "but all of the others eventually came down."

O ld-time Yankee teammates remembered Babe Ruth as much for his late-night barroom adventures as for his heroics on the field. At Ruth's funeral, on a blistering-hot August day, Waite Hoyt and Joe Dugan stood uncomfortably beneath the broiling sun. "I sure could go for a beer," said Hoyt. "So could the Babe," said Dugan.

T he immortal King Kelly was almost as famous for his feats of endurance in the barroom as for his prowess on the baseball diamond. While on a world tour in the 1890s, Kelly was complimenting a British reporter on the quality of the many London pubs he'd visited. A bit shocked, the reporter asked, "You don't drink while playing baseball, do you?" "It depends," said Kelly, "on the length of the game."

✳

I t was once suggested to Dodger pitcher Billy Loes that since he was the sole support of his parents, he should have some life insurance. "They wouldn't need it," said Billy. "If anything happened to me, it would kill 'em."

✳

O ld-time NHL referee Mickey Ion's credo was that "tough" was the only way to keep a game under control. And he proved it many times over. Ion once hit the young Toe Blake with a two-minute minor penalty and Blake was not inclined to accept it gracefully. As he skated past Mickey to the penalty box he fumed, "I can't tell you what I'd *like* to say, but if you could *guess* what I'm thinking . . ." "I *guessed* it," said Ion. "And that gets you *five* minutes!"

I t was another classic Ohio State-Michigan battle to decide just about everything, with the Wolverines winning by a touchdown. Did Woody Hayes take any comfort in the fact that his Buckeyes outgained Michigan by a goodly margin? "Statistics," said Hayes, "always remind me of the fellow who drowned in the river whose average depth was only three feet."

✳

I f there was a specific time when the Dodgers truly earned their reputation for zaniness, it had to be during the early 1930s when the old three-runners-on-third-base-at-the-same-time trick typified their antics. The players themselves seemed blissfully unconcerned about hovering near the bottom of the standings. A Brooklyn writer summed up their attitude quite nicely when he said, "Overconfidence may cost this team seventh place."

✳

O utfielder Taft Wright's problems on the field once made him the star of a Lefty Gomez story. Lefty, after looking at two strikes, hit a weak fly ball that Wright dropped. "Just the old Gomez strategy," said Lefty. "Take two and hit to Wright."

O ne of the embarrassments of early televised baseball was that when the TV camera peered into the dugout, it invariably found someone scratching. The good news, in case you haven't noticed, is that the boys on the bench have cleaned up their act. Somewhat. One who did notice was former Kansas City manager Jim Frey's daughter. When asked what her daddy did for a living, she replied, "I don't know; all I ever see him do is spit."

I s it possible that former Chicago Bears linebacker Dick Butkus was as ferocious and mean as everyone said he was? Let's hear it from Richard himself. "I never actually set out to hurt anybody," says Butkus, "unless it was really important . . . like a league game or something."

E ven though the Masters Champions Dinner was Ben Hogan's idea, he seems to have had some second thoughts about it. The traditional affair is held on the Tuesday night before the tournament opens. The previous year's winner selects the menu and picks up the tab for all the former Masters champions in attendance. "When I discovered that the cost of the dinner was more than the prize," said Ben, "I finished second four times."

T exas Tech coach J. T. King shared with all football coaches their mortal fear of the interception. During a tight game with SMU he sent an end in with a play that called for a sideline pass. "Tell him to throw it to you if you're open," said King, "and to me if you're not."

✳

I t was during the mid-1920s and once again the New York Yankees were running away with the American League pennant. Five or six of the Cleveland Indians, mired deep in seventh place, were sitting around a hotel lobby discussing New York's dominance. One of them allowed as how he'd sure love to play on that Yankee team. Another heartily agreed. So did a third and a fourth. Finally, Riggs Stephenson spoke up. "Boys," he said, "it seems to me that if *we* were all on the Yankees . . . *they'd* be in seventh place."

✳

I s violence getting out of hand in hockey? Is the game getting to be known more for scuffles than for skating? Comedian Rodney Dangerfield seems to think so. "I went to a fight the other night," says Rodney, "and a hockey game broke out."

Michigan State had just upset the powerful 1972 version of the Ohio State Buckeyes, but coach Duffy Daugherty was in for a test of his principles. His Dutch import soccer-style kicker, playing in his first college football game, had booted four field goals and had won the game. But during the locker room celebration the boy had asked Duffy for a light for his cigarette and then told Duffy and some reporters that his plan for the evening included "a lot of beer and a lot of girls." After a slight pause Duffy smiled weakly and said, "We have special rules for guys who kick four field goals."

Shortly after pitcher Don Drysdale had exchanged his mound duties for those of an announcer, Gene Mauch was asked to evaluate Drysdale's performance up in the booth. "He talks pretty good," said Mauch, "for a guy who spent most of his life with two fingers in his mouth."

According to Red Auerbach, Julius "Dr. J." Erving's success on the basketball court comes from his ability to keep one eye on the basket and one eye on his man. But the Doctor disagrees. "I keep both eyes on my man," says Erving. "The basket hasn't moved on me yet."

H ow does a catcher hang on to the elusive knuckleball? Former backstop Charlie Lau put it rather nicely. "There are two ways to catch a knuckleball," said Lau. "Unfortunately, neither of them works."

Few baseball teams in major league history were as futile as Casey Stengel's 1962 New York Mets. They won a mere 40 games (losing 120) and had losing streaks of 17 and 13 games . . . snatching many a defeat from the jaws of victory. Hearing that they'd scored eighteen runs in the previous night's game, one long-suffering Mets fan asked, "Did they win?"

Whitey Ford was one of those locker room wits not given nearly enough credit for that talent by the outside world. He was on the mound in a tight ball game when outfielder Hector Lopez made one of those diving, somersaulting miracle grabs that undoubtedly saved the game. Trooping into the clubhouse at the end of the game, Whitey palmed a make-believe microphone to "interview" Lopez. "Tell us, Hector," he said, "when did you first realize that you'd misjudged the ball."

The remarkable Willie Shoemaker's long career as a brilliant jockey is a classic sports story. What was his secret for such longevity and success? A rival jockey thinks it had something to do with Willie's rapport with his horses. "All riders talk to their horses," he says, "but Shoemaker's the only one the horses talked back to."

J ames "Cool Papa" Bell was one of the legends in the old Negro leagues; he was known especially for his speed on the base paths. Teammate Satchel Paige had a few colorful, if questionable, descriptions of Bell's fleetness of foot. "He was so fast," said Satch, "that when he flipped the wall switch in a hotel room, he'd be in bed before the light went out." Satchel also maintained that Cool Papa once hit a grounder back through the middle and as he slid into second he was hit by his own batted ball.

✳

E arly in his sports career football coach Shug Jordan gave up pitching baseball and turned to the gridiron. When did the moment of decision come? "One day I threw my best fastball and hit a guy right between the eyes," said Jordan. "It didn't even faze him. He just tossed his bat away and trotted down to first. I decided right then that it was time to quit."

✳

B illy Graham is almost as avid about his golf game as he is about saving souls. But apparently, he keeps his two major interests separate. "Prayer never seems to work for me on the golf course," says Graham. "I think this has something to do with my being a terrible putter."

D uring the 1970 World Series, Baltimore's Brooks Robinson put on a special show for the rival Cincinnati Reds. He treated them to an incredible fielding exhibition, making one spectacular play after another—many at the expense of Johnny Bench, the Reds' catcher. Later, after Robinson had won the new car that goes with the Series' MVP Award, Bench, a car dealer on the side, said, "If we'd known he wanted a car *that* badly, we'd have *given* him one."

✳

I n the days of much higher batting averages, Lefty Gomez's statistics bear out his claims of futility at the plate. His lifetime regular season average was an anemic .147, and throughout his many World Series his mark was a mere .150. But as Lefty points out, there is a difference. "I always hit better in the Series," he explains.

✳

I n spite of idle gossip to the contrary, Big Daddy Lipscomb *did* have a method to his style of defensive line-play when he was with the Colts and the Steelers. "I grab me a whole armful of guys with the other color jersey," said Big Daddy. "Then I peel 'em off till I find the one with the ball."

M uch-traveled second baseman Ron Hunt didn't have to apologize to anyone for his skills with either bat or glove. But one of his more artistic talents was his uncanny knack for getting knicked by the pitch. (In 1971 he was hit by the pitcher fifty times, leading the league in that department by a margin of forty-one "hits.") His fine sense of timing and a baggy uniform were two of the tools he employed in getting hit without getting hurt. The Montreal Expos' press guide once summed up Ron's rare talent rather nicely. "Ron gets good skin on the ball," it said.

D uring spring training in St. Petersburg one year, Pepper Martin complained about the Cardinals' two-a-day workouts, citing the more casual schedule of the Yankees across town. Manager Ray Blades explained that when the Cardinals got to be as good as the Yankees, he'd ease up on them. "I got a jackass back in Oklahoma," said Martin, "and you can work him from dawn till dusk and he still ain't never gonna win the Kentucky Derby."

W hen Darrell Dawkins went on his slam-dunk backboard-smashing binge, Atlanta officials were prepared for him. "We can get a new backboard up in just thirty-five minutes . . . unless the framework is bent," said one. Can a human being bend a steel frame like that? "No human can," said the official, "but Dawkins might be able to."

Frank Szymanski was a very good center for the Chicago Bears. He was also a very modest man. Thus it came as a surprise that when testifying as a character witness, he identified himself, in answer to a question, as the world's best center. Asked later by a friend about why he'd given that answer, he said, "I had to. I was under oath."

✳

Back when he was getting the Oakland Raider franchise started, Al Davis heard that Nicky Hilton had made a quick $100,000 in Los Angeles baseball. True? Well, not quite. First of all, according to Hilton, it was his brother, not he. And it was San Diego, not L.A. And football, not baseball. And $1 million, not $100,000. And he didn't make it, he lost it.

✳

Ask any group of American men what they plan to do when they retire and the vast majority will tell you they want to fish and play golf. Of course, there are those few who don't even *want* to retire. Like long-time golf pro Julius Boros. "Why would I want to retire?" asked Boros, late in his career. "All I do *now* is fish and play golf."

Years ago a Big Ten football game ended with Iowa edging Purdue by the unusual score of 4–0. Said ever-confident Iowa coach Eddie Anderson, "We had it clinched with that first safety, but we wanted to run up the score."

When Freddie Patek was asked how it felt to be, at only 5 feet 4 inches, the shortest player in the major leagues, he said, "A heckuva lot better than being the shortest player in the minor leagues."

Coach Don Shula has spent so many years at the helm of the Miami Dolphins that some football fans might forget that he once coached the Baltimore Colts. Thus it was ironic when Shula's son, Dave, was drafted out of Dartmouth . . . by the Baltimore Colts. Sportswriter Will Browning thought there was much more to it, though. "This completes the deal in which Don Shula went from Baltimore to Miami," said Browning. "In return, the Colts were to get his firstborn son."

W hen John Mariucci was coaching the U.S. Olympic hockey team, there was a time or two when he became a bit impatient with his young and inexperienced squad. During one locker room tirade he screamed, "Every day you guys look worse and worse. And today you played like tomorrow!"

✳

E x-Brigham Young University All-American Danny Ainge got the basketball bug early in life and worked hard at perfecting his game. How hard? Let's hear it from Danny's father Don about the time he put up a hoop for eight-year-old Danny and his brothers. "They wore out four baskets," says Don Ainge. "And I don't mean nets, I mean *rims*."

✳

S atchel Paige never believed in wasting energy on nonessentials, like conditioning exercises. Once, with the old St. Louis Browns, manager Rogers Hornsby took Satch aside and said, "You and I are a couple of old-timers and we've got to show these kids how to train. We should set a good example by *working* hard." "Only trouble is," said Satch, "that *one* of us old-timers also got to *pitch*."

J oe Kelly once suffered the same fate that many rookies experience in spring training—tearing the cover off the ball until the pitchers start to catch up. Upon being demoted to Toronto he was stopped by immigration officials and asked the standard question: "How long do you expect to stay in Canada?" "Until they start throwing curve balls," replied Kelly.

✳

N ever argue with Yogi Berra when cool, clear logic is needed to answer a difficult question. Several players were discussing the possibility of special promotions increasing attendance for one of the league's weaker teams. Yogi contended that that sort of thing wouldn't matter. "If the fans don't want to come out," he explained, "nobody can stop 'em."

✳

T here are some baseball teams in places like Japan and Cuba who question the accuracy of the term *World Series*. But, as usual, George Steinbrenner clarified the matter. After a Series victory George was asked how the Yankees could claim the world championship when the only teams represented were from Canada and the United States. "We beat everybody who showed up," he said.

A s long and as illustrious as Roger Staubach's career was, he never got to call his own plays in the huddle. An emissary from coach Tom Landry came trotting in from the bench with the appropriate instructions. Once, after a faltering start on a football banquet speech, he paused and explained. "I keep waiting for Mike Ditka or Bill Truax to bring in the words," he said.

＊

P ro golfers make more money than most of the people who watch them, but sometimes there's an advantage in being the spectator. At least, Johnny Miller felt that way after shooting a front-nine 39 at the 1975 Crosby. "If I had been in the gallery," said Miller, "I'd have gone home."

＊

W hen Alex Johnson was with the Cincinnati Reds, he was not the world's most coopera-tive interviewee. But you certainly couldn't fault him on his math. Early in the year a reporter asked him, "Alex, you hit only two homers all last year and this season you already have seven—what's the difference?" "Five," said Alex.

ack when Muhammad Ali was just plain Cassius Clay and loudly proclaiming that he was the greatest, he didn't necessarily limit the claim to the ring. When asked how he was at golf, he replied, "I'm the best. I just haven't played yet."

L efty Gomez once shocked the entire baseball world by slashing out a legitimate two-base hit. He slid dramatically into second, dusted himself off with a flourish, and glanced smugly over at the Yankee bench. Then he tugged at his cap, took a short lead, and promptly got picked off. He was met at the bench by a fuming manager Joe McCarthy, who growled, "Dammit, Gomez, is that any way to act on second base!" "How should I know?" said Gomez. "I've never been there before."

I t sometimes takes a new football coach several years to get things going his way. And that often involves more than just his "system." Cal Stoll gave us a good example while he was coaching at the University of Minnesota. "This year we've got Nebraska right where we want 'em," said Stoll. "Off the schedule."

T he traditional baseball hierarchy never seemed to welcome maverick Bill Veeck into its owners' ranks. One reason might have been that old Bill wasn't too subtle in his appraisal of his fellow magnates. "He's the only guy I know," said Veeck of one of the other owners, "whom Will Rogers would punch right in the mouth."

W ith its cozy left field dimensions, Boston's Fenway Park has always been a graveyard for pitchers. Especially left-handers. But back in the 1930s Lefty Gomez, one of the foremost southpaws of his day, tried to outpsych the old bandbox ball park. When visiting manager Joe McCarthy arrived at Fenway one day, he found Gomez sitting in a phone booth outside the park. "I'm staying in here right until game time," said Lefty. "Then when I get in there, the place'll seem huge."

G etting a football team psyched up for a game gives them a leg up, right? That's how coach Chuck Mills felt, even though his U.S. Merchant Marine team had just been clobbered by Bucknell, 37–0. "Fortunately, we were really up for the game," said Mills. "Otherwise, they'd have killed us."

S ubtlety was never one of Dave Bristol's strong points, and he proved it while managing the San Francisco Giants. Addressing the team after a poorly played loss on the road, he said, "There'll be two buses leaving the hotel for tomorrow night's game. The two P.M. bus will be for those of you who need a little extra work. The empty bus will leave at five P.M."

Lefty Gomez, with his famous .147 lifetime batting average, had one big chance for fame as a hitter. But he claims that his battery mate, Bill Dickey, blew it for him. It was in the 1934 All-Star Game when, as everyone knows, Carl Hubbell struck out five American League sluggers in a row: Ruth, Gehrig, Foxx, Simmons, and Cronin. But few remember that, after Cronin, Dickey singled and Gomez then fanned. "If Dickey had only struck out," says Gomez, "I'd be in the record book with all those other great hitters."

An aversion to physical contact is not one of the qualities you look for in a running back, so Bob Newhart probably made the right decision in becoming a comedian. Describing his brief high school career as a halfback, Newhart says, "When I went into the line on a fake, I'd holler, 'I don't have it, I don't have it!'"

In an obviously token effort to provide equal time for a less than avid opinion of sports, we turn the podium over to former senator and presidential candidate Gene McCarthy. "Politics is like coaching football," said McCarthy. "You have to be smart enough to know the game, and dumb enough to think it's important."

Most golfers, at some extreme point of frustration, have actually thrown a club . . . or even stalked angrily off the course in the middle of a round. But few have brought it off with the style of England's formidable Viscount Castlerosse back in the 1930s. One day, after topping three straight shots, he had turned toward the clubhouse, smoldering with rage. But then, with remarkable composure, he paused, gestured toward the ball, and calmly instructed his caddie to, "Pick that up, have the clubs destroyed, and leave the course."

During the mid-1970s Jack Nicklaus reigned as the undisputed king of the golf world. But Tom Weiskopf, for one, wasn't overawed by the Golden Bear. "I'm not afraid of Jack," said Weiskopf. "If you play better than he does, you can beat him."

How much weight can a pitcher lose in a game when he has to toil under the hot Texas sun? Five pounds . . . ten . . . twenty? Not very much at all, if you happen to be tall, skinny Jim Kern, who pitched for the Rangers. "How much can bones sweat?" asks Kern.

Was pitcher Bill "Spaceman" Lee unhappy about leaving the Boston Red Sox after the 1978 season, which saw the Sox blow a fourteen-game lead? Apparently not. "Who wants to be on a team that goes down in history with the 'sixty-four Phillies and the 'sixty-seven Arabs?" said Lee.

T he coach of any expansion team has to be a patient, long-suffering type, prepared to endure many indignities. When Bep Guidolin was coaching the fledgling Kansas City Scouts, he was asked whether the team's inept play caused him any nightmares. "Not really," said Guidolin, "you have to sleep to have nightmares."

✳

H all of Fame third baseman Pie Traynor was as great on the field as he was at the plate. Once, while injured, he had to sit and suffer as his rookie replacement made ten errors in three games. Then, rushed back into the lineup, Traynor booted the first ball that came to him. Coming to the bench after the inning, Traynor was heard to grumble, "That kid's got third base so screwed up nobody can play it."

✳

W hen Al Denson was a wide receiver with the Denver Broncos, he explained what it's like to know you're going to get clobbered the moment you touch a pass. "It's like walking out of a grocery store with a bag full of groceries and getting hit by a car," said Denson. "Sometimes you don't care what happens to the groceries."

L efty Gomez lived in mortal fear of burly Red Sox slugger Jimmy Foxx. Once, with Lefty on the mound, Foxx dug in at the plate in a ninth-inning, bases-loaded, score-tied situation. Gomez shook off four straight signals and finally catcher Bill Dickey dropped his mask and went to the mound. "What's going on," said Dickey, "I've called every pitch you know how to throw!" "Let's not be in any big hurry," said Gomez. "Maybe he'll get a phone call or something."

✳

H ow bad a hitter *was* Lefty Gomez? Let's hear it from the great Yankee pitcher himself. "If you were to run by me, I couldn't hit you with a bat," says Lefty. But then, after a moment's reflection on the subject, he adds, "Oh, I might foul you *off*, but I wouldn't hit you."

✳

I t was late in the game, back in the days when relief pitchers were a rare breed, and Lefty Gomez was starting to fade. Yankee catcher Bill Dickey came to the mound to suggest that Lefty try to put a little more on his fastball. "I'm throwing it just as hard as ever," protested Gomez. "It's just not getting there as soon."

B ack in the days when $20,000 was a superstar salary, Babe Ruth staggered the sports world by holding out for $80,000 one spring. A reporter pointed out that that was more than President Hoover was making. The Babe thought about that for a minute and then replied, "Maybe so, but I had a better year than he did."

✳

R on Fairly, still with the California Angels at the age of thirty-nine, stoutly maintained that he hadn't lost a bit of speed on the base paths over the years. The reason? "There wasn't anything there to lose," he said.

✳

D uring his career as an NHL coach, no one ever accused Gerry Cheevers of taking the game too lightly. But that wasn't always the case. During his rookie year as a goalie for the Boston Bruins, Cheevers was once creamed by the Blackhawks, 10–2. "Dammit," screamed Boston general manager Hap Emms after the slaughter, "what *happened* out there!" Without missing a beat, Cheevers replied, "Roses are red, violets are blue, they got ten, we got two."

When MacArthur Lane was a running back for the Green Bay Packers, he had the dubious privilege of facing the Bears and their ferocious linebacker, Dick Butkus. Twice a year, yet. And he didn't seem to enjoy Butkus's imaginative approach to the game. "One time he bit me," said Lane. "Another time he tried to break my leg, but nothing happened. I guess maybe the leg was too green."

Radio broadcaster Frank Messer saw the longest home run ever hit by mighty old-time slugger Luke Easter. Or at least, he *thought* he did. After the game he described to Easter just how far he'd seen it go from his rooftop broadcast booth at Buffalo's old Offerman Stadium. "I saw it all the way," said the excited Messer. "If you saw it all the way," said Easter, "it ain't the longest ball ol' Luke ever hit."

Hockey coaches are much like coaches in any other sport. For all but a rare few, being hired is just a step on the way to being fired. Wren Blair said it rather well when, as Pittsburgh Penguin president, he was asked whether his new coach was an interim coach. "Aren't all coaches interim coaches?" he asked.

I n 1967, with the Baltimore Bullets deep in last place, coach Gene Shue was complaining about the series of bad breaks and injuries that had plagued the team. "The way things are going," he said, "we could get Wilt Chamberlain in a trade and then find out he's really two midgets Scotch-taped together."

Many baseball managers agonize over their pitching rotation for the series ahead or for the week ahead. Or even for the *season* ahead. Leo Durocher made it simple. You just looked around to see who was ready, was his philosophy. "You don't save a pitcher for tomorrow," said Leo. "It might rain tomorrow."

✳

Woody Hayes had been around long enough to know that Dame Fortune is a fickle lady, indeed. And so are football fans. "They'll give you the new Cadillac one year," said Woody, "and the next year they give you the gas to get out of town."

✳

Sometimes it isn't what you do *or* whom you know. It just might be how you *look* at things. As when Hot Rod Hundley tells of his biggest thrill while playing for the Los Angeles Lakers. "It was the night that Elgin Baylor and I combined for seventy-three points," says Hundley. "Elgin had seventy-one of them."

W hen Dick Butkus starred for the Chicago Bears, his chief claim to fame was his ferocious play. But in case you were keeping track and wondered why Butkus was awarded so few game balls, Alex Hawkins is ready to enlighten you. "Whenever they gave Butkus the game ball," says Hawkins, "he ate it."

✳

S ome ballplayers vent their frustrations and anger with physical outbursts—kicking the water cooler or banging a locker or throwing things. Of the "throwing things" group, former catcher Ed Bailey rates the late Freddie Hutchinson the clear winner. "Some guys throw stools," says Bailey. "Hutch threw rooms."

✳

I t was one thing to knock down old-time boxer Stanley Ketchel. It was quite another thing to keep him down. On those rare occasions when he did suffer the indignity of being decked, he usually came off the canvas in a rage. An incredulous friend, hearing of Ketchel's death, offered a suggestion. "Stand over him and start counting," he said. "He'll get up at nine."

W hen Dodger pitcher Claude Osteen heard that he'd been offered to the then-lowly California Angels in a trade, he was insulted. He was doubly insulted. "I'm not sure which is worse," he said, "being offered or having the trade turned down."

※

T om Brock was the football coach at the University of Omaha when he came up with his own definition of what makes a successful coach. "A good coach is one who can be chased down the street by irate alumni," said Brock, "and make it look like he's leading a parade."

※

P rimo Carnera was the hulking giant who captured the boxing world's imagination during the 1930s. Not much on defensive skills, he seemed willing to absorb a hundred punches if he could get off one good one himself. It was during his fight with Max Baer, with Baer giving Primo a thorough boxing lesson, that Grantland Rice remarked, "The big fellow sure can take it." "Yes," said another writer, Heywood Broun, "but he doesn't seem to know what to do with it."

Before the Pittsburgh Steelers won all those Super Bowls, things weren't always run in first-class fashion. A veteran remembers the equipment manager, during one dismal training camp, announcing, "Okay, good news. Today everybody gets a change of T-shirts. Mansfield, you change with Van Dyke. Russell, you change with . . ."

✳

Pepper Rodgers's UCLA football team had had a terrible season and, as coach, he was taking a lot of heat. "My dog was about my only friend, and I told my wife that a man *needs* at least *two* friends," says Rodgers. "She bought me another dog."

✳

When Joe McCarthy managed the Chicago Cubs during the early 1930s, he took on the additional task of trying to reform high-living outfielder Hack Wilson. McCarthy began with a demonstration. He dropped a live worm into a glass of water and the worm just wiggled around. Then he put the same worm into a glass of gin and, as Wilson watched, the worm died. "What does that prove to you, Hack?" asked McCarthy. "It proves that if you drink gin you won't have worms," said Wilson.

H urdler Eddie Ottoz was always more concerned with getting a good jump at the gun than he was with being perfectly groomed at race time. Ottoz, who happened to be Italian, explained why he always competed without shaving beforehand. "Italian men and Russian women never shave before a meet," he said.

C onfidence in your own decisions is all-important to sports officials. And King Kong Klein, a football and basketball star at New York University during the 1930s, never lacked that quality when he became a referee. Once, calling a contact foul in a basketball game, he heard the culprit protest, "Hey, I never touched him!" "Well then you should have," said Klein, "because that's the way I called it."

✳

I n case you've ever been tempted to complain about the heat, here's some reassurance from coach Tom Landry. It was during a Dallas Cowboy workout and the temperature was over 100 degrees. For some faltering Cowboy stalwarts, Landry clarified the matter. "The heat is entirely mental," he explained. "It's only when you pass out that it becomes physical."

✳

A mong Leo Durocher's qualities as a baseball manager was his total and unqualified confidence in his own decisions and strategies. When one of his coaches cautioned him to consider some possible unforseen developments in a particular game, Leo responded, "There ain't gonna *be* any unforseen."

When Fresco Thompson was scouting for the Dodgers, he went to Cuba for a look at hot prospect Minnie Minoso. He stayed long enough to see Minoso make a couple of boneheaded plays in the field and then caught a plane home. A few years later, as Minoso was becoming the batting sensation of the American League, Thompson was heard to lament, "I guess intellect isn't everything in this game. They say Einstein wasn't much of a hitter."

Clyde Lovellette was one of the NBA's big scoring threats for a number of years. But he never threatened *anyone* on defense—a point that Paul Seymour stressed when presenting Lovellette with a scoring award. "Here it is, Clyde, a trophy commemorating your twenty-five thousand points," said Seymour, "the ten thousand you've scored and the fifteen thousand you've given up."

Yogi Berra's irrefutable logic just seems to get better and better. Asked by a waitress whether he wanted his pizza cut into four pieces or eight, Yogi replied, "Better make it four . . . I don't think I can eat eight."

O ne of pro football linebacker Pete Wysocki's 1980 New Year's resolutions was to *do* something about the monotonous succession of "Hi, Mom"s and "We're number one"s that the TV viewer is subjected to whenever the camera goes in tight on the bench. "I'm going to say hello to a cousin and claim that we're number four," said Wysocki.

✳

P ete Rose always grabbed more than his share of the spotlight. And that was too bad, because his wife Karolyn was worth watching, too. And listening to. On her Cincinnati radio talk show Karolyn once referred to the start of a hockey game as "the puck-off."

✳

I t was 1972 and Jack Kent Cooke was deeply disappointed at the sparse crowds coming out to watch his NHL Los Angeles Kings. That was especially strange, a reporter pointed out, because there were, at that time, some 800,000 ex-Canadians living in the Los Angeles area. "I've just discovered why they left Canada," said Cooke. "They hate hockey."

G ood-hit-terrible-field Babe Herman was very upset with a reporter who suggested that the Babe had recently fielded some fly balls with his head. "I promise you this," said Herman, "if I ever get hit on the head by a fly ball I'll walk off the field and never come back." "How about getting hit on the shoulder, Babe?" asked the reporter. Herman thought for a moment and then said, "Oh, no, on the shoulder don't count."

✳

W hen you're hot, you're hot, is the way Lee Trevino feels about it. Back in 1973 Trevino was on a roll and, referring to the custom of a pro golfer giving his caddie a percentage of his winnings, he said, "I'm going to win so much this year that my *caddie* will make the top twenty money winners list."

✳

W hen Sam Bailey was coaching football at Tampa University, he had mixed feelings about a big interior lineman he was trying to recruit. "He's as big as a gorilla and as strong as a gorilla," said Bailey. "Now if he were as *smart* as a gorilla, he'd be fine."

T wo masters of their sports, Ted Williams and Sam Snead, were discussing the relative difficulties of their games. Williams suggested that nothing could be tougher than hitting a baseball coming at you at 100 miles per hour. "Maybe so," said Snead, "but you don't have to go into the stands and play your foul balls like we do."

Early Wynn was mean out there on the mound, and every hitter knew that digging in on him was a clear invitation for a fastball up under the chin. A reporter once asked Wynn if it were true that, in a crucial situation, he would knock down his own mother. "I guess I would," he said after a pause, "but only if she were really crowding the plate."

✷

Some athletes are known for their violent outbursts and temper tantrums. But golfer Jimmy Demaret had a nomination for the player with the most *even* temperament. "It was Clayton Haefner," said Demaret. "He was mad *all* the time."

✷

Ex-catcher Bob Uecker contends that his most difficult task ever was trying to handle Phil Niekro's elusive knuckler. "If he was throwing it hard," says Uecker, "I'd just start running and play it off the backstop. Otherwise, I'd simply follow it till it stopped rolling and then pick it up."

Does the "free ride" that many college athletes get include freedom from such bothersome details as books and studying? Well, we *think* Marlin McKeever was kidding when, during a homecoming tour of the USC campus, he said, "Gee, this is exciting. I've never *been* in one of these classrooms before."

✳

Pitcher Bob Muncrief had just served up a curve ball to Ralph Kiner and the Pittsburgh slugger had lost it in the left field bleachers. After the inning Cubs manager Frankie Frisch told Muncrief, "Never give Kiner a curve. Throw him nothing but fastballs." Next time up, Kiner hit Muncrief's first fastball about eight miles. As Frisch came to the mound, Muncrief said, "Well, Frank, he hit yours a lot farther than he hit mine."

✳

A reporter was asking pro quarterback Ken Stabler about adventure writer Jack London's philosophy. It read, in part, "I would rather be ashes than dust. I would rather that my spark should burn out in a brilliant blaze than it should be stifled by dry rot. I would rather be a superb meteor than a sleepy, permanent planet." What did all that mean? "Throw deep," said Stabler.

E arly in the 1940 NFL title game between Washington and Chicago, a Redskins end dropped a sure touchdown pass from quarterback Sammy Baugh. The Bears then went on to crush the Skins 73–0. Later, a reporter asked Baugh if that early lost touchdown would have changed the outcome of the game. "Sure it would have," said Sammy. "The score would have been seventy-three to seven."

✳

E verybody has to start somewhere. Hall of Fame catcher Gabby Hartnett had just been called up from the Cubs' Woonsocket, Rhode Island, farm club and was having a shaky first inning behind the plate. "What's the matter, kid," asked the ump, "is this the first big league game you've caught?" "Mister," said Hartnett, "this is the first big league game I've *seen*."

✳

W hen Joe Cantillon managed the old Minneapolis Millers, he recommended the team's Kansas City hotel to a friend going there. Later, the friend complained that he had awakened during the night to see a huge rat carrying off one of his socks. "Well, if you had told them you were my friend," said Cantillon, "they'd have put a cat in your room."

I t's easy for us armchair quarterbacks to look back on a botched play and decide, very sagely, "what the guy shoulda done." But the man down on the field has to make his decisions instantaneously. When critics disagreed with what kick returner Steve Wilson did with a muffed punt, his response was both honest and apt. "I didn't know the rule," said Wilson, "and I didn't have time to look it up."

B asketball's Bill Russell had a lot of talent . . . and a lot of pride, too. Because their careers didn't overlap, a reporter once asked Russell how he would have done against Kareem Abdul-Jabbar. "Young man," said Russell, "you have the question backwards."

※

F rankie Frisch had his own theatrical ways of irritating a longtime adversary, umpire Bill Klem. Once, as Klem called a third strike on one of his hitters, Frisch, standing in the third base coaching box, screamed in anguish and fell to the ground, twitching violently. It was the last straw for Klem. As he started down the line, he yelled, "Frank, if you're not dead when I get there, you're out of the game!"

※

E ven when Dizzy Dean was at his best, the Giants' Bill Terry hit him with monotonous regularity. In one game Terry sent three straight line drives screaming back through the mound, narrowly missing Dean each time. After the third one Pepper Martin called time and strolled over with some advice for Dean. "Jerome," he said, "I don't think you're playin' Terry deep enough."

D oes he or doesn't he? What about mixing sex with sports—does it really hurt an athlete's performance? Old philosopher Casey Stengel had his own theory. "It isn't sex that wrecks these guys," said Casey. "It's staying up all night looking for it."

✳

W hen ex-Marine Hank Bauer became a manager, he had some pretty rigid rules for his team. Two of them were that the manager didn't fraternize with the players and that, when on the road, the players could not drink in the team hotel's bar. Was he concerned about the players scandalizing the hotel's other patrons? "No," said Bauer, "that's where I do *my* drinking."

✳

D izzy Dean was pretty proud of a home run he once hit for Houston in the Texas League. It was, in fact, still the game's *only* run when Dean's wildness got him into trouble in the seventh inning. Miffed at being removed from the game, he ran to the scoreboard and took down the "1." "If you ain't gonna let me pitch," he yelled in to the bench, "then I ain't gonna let you have my run!"

I f you think Yogi Berra takes the game of baseball lightly, you are gravely mistaken. The evidence that he believes the game can be analyzed with mathematical precision came when he was heard explaining to a teammate, "Ninety percent of this game is half-mental."

M anager-general manager Joe Engel was once having trouble signing a young player for his Chattanooga club. Finally the youngster wired Engel an ultimatum: DOUBLE YOUR OFFER OR COUNT ME OUT. Engel fired off a return telegram that read simply: 1-2-3-4-5-6-7-8-9-10.

R ed Ruffing enjoyed many years with all that famous Yankee power behind him. But it was a different story when, as a youngster, he was with the Red Sox. During one game *against* the Yankees, Ruffing was in the bull pen and had just started a sandwich when the call came for him to come in in relief. "Who's coming up?" he asked. Someone said, "Ruth, Gehrig, and Meusel." "Don't anyone touch that sandwich," said Ruffing. "I'll be right back."

S hortly after Pepper Rodgers had been named the football coach at UCLA, his wife had to admonish their young boy not to run around their new neighborhood telling everyone that he was the son of the new coach. As mother and son emerged from church the following Sunday, the minister introduced himself and asked the boy who his daddy was. "I thought it was Pepper Rodgers," the boy said, "but Mom says it isn't."

H ow does a lifetime .300 hitter get humility? Offer him this bit of insight from an anonymous baseball sage. "Let's say you play fifteen years, bat six thousand times and get two thousand hits," he said. "That's a .333 average and that's pretty good. But you could also think of it as going oh for four thousand."

G eorge Allen was always willing to expend all his energies, and anything else that was required, including money, to build a winning football team. Washington Redskins owner Edward Bennett Williams confirmed that shortly after Allen had taken over the team. "I have given him an unlimited budget," said Williams, "and he's already exceeded it."

N obody seems to be neutral on Reggie Jackson. You're either a fan or a detractor. And one-time teammate Darold Knowles would seem to be in the latter camp. "There isn't enough mustard in the world to cover Reggie Jackson," he says.

Wilbert Robinson, of the old Dodgers, came to the mound one day to remove a pitcher who was getting shelled. The pitcher protested loudly, however, and while they argued, the right fielder, Babe Herman, decided to lie down and rest for a moment. Then the pitcher, angrily heading for the bench, turned and fired the ball at the right field wall. Herman, thinking the assault had started again, leaped up, grabbed the carom and threw a strike to second base. Robinson shook his head in wonder. "Best damn throw he's made all year," he said.

✳

Richie Scheinblum started his big league career with the Cleveland Indians and then moved on to what he obviously considered greener pastures. "The only good thing about playing for Cleveland," said Richie, "is that you don't have to go there on road trips."

✳

Actor Chuck Connors once played some major league baseball and we are indebted to him for explaining Branch Rickey's tight-fisted fiscal policies when they were both with the Dodgers. "Rickey had both money and players," said Connors. "He just didn't like to see the two of them mix."

During a Los Angeles Rams training camp scrimmage, fleet halfback Glenn Davis returned a kickoff 95 yards for a score. An assistant coach immediately took him aside to explain all the things he'd done wrong: his cuts, not following his blockers, carrying the ball in the wrong hand, and so on. When he finished, Davis said, "How was it for distance, coach?"

✳

In a world where there are fewer and fewer certainties, it's good to know that you can count on chess player Bobby Fischer. One would never expect Mr. Fischer to be a shrinking violet, and one is not disappointed. Asked about his claim that he is the only immortal player in the world today, he responds, "It's nice to be modest, but it's stupid not to tell the truth."

✳

During his long career as a general manager, Frank Lane was well known for his wheeling and dealing, for his frequent and often unexpected trades. Once, while with the hapless Milwaukee Brewers, he returned from the winter meetings where, much to everyone's surprise, he hadn't made a single trade. "We didn't want to weaken the rest of the league," Lane explained.

I n his entire baseball career, Bobby Thomson was thrown out of only one game. That happened when, after a questionable called strike, Thomson turned and quietly inquired about umpire Augie Donatelli's ancestry. Later, Thomson asked Donatelli why he'd got so upset. "After all," said Thomson, "only you and the catcher heard what I'd said." "True," said Donatelli, "but I didn't want that catcher going through life thinking that about me."

M ark Twain was not an avid golf fan, but he was quite a student of human nature. So golfers everywhere have the benefit of a bit of sardonic advice from the legendary wit. "It is not considered good sportsmanship," said Twain, "to pick up lost golf balls while they are still rolling."

S outhern Methodist University basketball coach Sonny Allen had a problem. He had some intense competition from other schools in recruiting a hot, all-state high school prospect who just happened to be his own son. A friend asked, facetiously, if Allen had considered offering the boy a car to come to SMU. "No," said Allen, "but I'm considering taking one away if he doesn't."

I f Pete Rose has any faults as a ballplayer, they are very difficult to detect. Therefore, if you're going to try to zap him somehow, it can't be on performance. So a group of roasters chose to attack him, good-naturedly, on another front: his intellect. Never mind that that might also be a shaky premise; they did get off some pretty good lines. "I'll tell you how smart Pete Rose is," said Reds announcer Joe Nuxhall. "When they had that last blackout in New York, Pete was stranded for thirteen hours . . . on an escalator."

✳

B efore Alex Karras turned to professional football, he played at Iowa. In fact, it seemed to Big Ten opponents that he played there for quite a while. But let's let Alex clear up the matter. "I played at Iowa for only two terms," he says, "Truman's and Eisenhower's."

✳

E very football player lives in fear of the crippling knee injury that can end his career on the spot. Knees, apparently, weren't invented with football in mind. E. J. Holub, the former Kansas City linebacker, threw in the towel only after a long series of operations. "My knees look like I lost a knife fight with a midget," said Holub.

M|any hockey players, especially the Canadian ones speak both English and French. But Gordie Howe contends that *all* pro athletes are bilingual. "They all speak English," says Gordie, "and profanity."

D on Zimmer and Buzzy Bavasi had some differences when Zimmer played for the Dodgers and Bavasi was the team's general manager. After one period of bench sitting, Zimmer presented Buzzy with the old familiar "play me or trade me" ultimatum. Bavasi tried to cooperate, but claimed that it didn't work out for anybody. "After we played him for a while and the other teams got another look at him, we couldn't trade him," said Bavasi.

✳

S ome baseball players are slow by nature. Like Ernie Lombardi, Cincinnati's great hulk of a catcher during the 1930s. Others just get that way after a while. Shortstop Lou Boudreau, brilliant as he was on the field, got slower and slower as his bad ankles got worse. Near the end of Boudreau's career, sportswriter Stanley Frank compared the two: "Boudreau is now the slowest ballplayer since Ernie Lombardi was thrown out at first trying to stretch a double into a single."

Football coach Lou Holtz may have some shortcomings, but a lack of confidence isn't one of them. Back when he signed to coach the New York Jets, he immediately started building a new home on Long Island. A reporter reminded him that, considering the insecurity of a coach's job, that seemed a bit optimistic. "Yes, it is," said Holtz. "It's like doing a crossword puzzle with a pen."

Jim Fuller was listening to a Houston Astro teammate predict his own accomplishments for the season ahead. The estimated numbers included twenty stolen bases and, apparently, Mr. Fuller did not share his colleague's confidence in his skill on the base paths. "The only way he'll steal twenty bases," said Fuller, "is to break into the equipment room."

Catcher Tim McCarver had just had the rare honor of having a stadium named after him back in his hometown of Memphis. A teammate asked him, however, why the place was called the Tim McCarver Memorial Stadium when, to all outward appearances, he was still very much alive. "They named it after my arm," said Mc-Carver.

As quarterback Sammy Baugh's great pro football career went on and on, he stoutly refused to be pinned down as to when he might hang up his cleats. But on the other hand, he was also realistic about the fragility of his aging bones. When, during the season, someone asked him once again if this might be his last year, Baugh replied, "I don't know. Maybe last year was."

The Canadian boxer, George Chuvalo, had just absorbed another severe beating and his manager, Irving Ungerman, was wondering aloud, to a group of sportswriters, whether he should let Chuvalo fight again. "Irving, if he's got one good punch left in him," said one of them, "he should throw it at you."

Any good budget should be flexible enough to accommodate a little unspecified fun and recreation. And Tug McGraw was ready to apply that principle when he became one of the first relief pitchers to start pulling down big bucks. "Ninety percent of the money I plan to spend on good times, women, and Irish whiskey," said McGraw. "But the other ten percent I'll probably just waste."

A manager can enhance his reputation for being a great sage only if his team is in frequent need of good advice. Casey Stengel needn't have worried. His lowly New York Mets teams of the early 1960s gave him plenty of opportunities to apply his words of wisdom. Once, when one of his young pitchers committed a balk because a fly landed on his nose, Casey was equal to the occasion. "Son, if you want to pitch in the big leagues," said Stengel, "you'll have to learn to catch those in your mouth."

T he NFL's syndicate scouting has developed the process of drafting college players into something of a science. All a team has to decide, on any given round, is whether to draft the best remaining player at a given position or to go for the best available athlete. Back before the computers got into the act, though, the Chicago Bears made their first draft choice someone they thought was a versatile player. The episode did *not* end happily. "He *is* a versatile guy," said a Bears assistant coach. "So far we've found six positions he can't play."

Even though he tolerated a good passing quarterback now and then, Woody Hayes was best known for his "three yards and a cloud of dust" offenses while at Ohio State. And although Woody probably best epitomizes that brand of coaching that concentrates on the running game, it was Duffy Daugherty who best summed up the antipassing philosophy. "Only three things can happen when you put the ball up in the air," said Duffy, "and two of them are bad."

It is probably safe to say that no one has ever accused sportscaster Howard Cosell of being overly modest. But few have ever expressed, head on, the opinion that the Great Man was *immodest*, either. Harry Markson is one of that select group. Hearing Cosell declare that there were not many truly great sports announcers working today, Markson said, "There's one fewer than you think there are, Howard."

The following argument about the merits of the modern hitter versus the old-time greats may never have actually happened, but we'd like to think it did.

First Man: Okay, wise guy, what do you think Ty *Cobb* would hit against today's pitching?
Second Man: Oh, maybe .320 or .325.
First Man: What's so great about *that*?
Second Man: Well, you've gotta remember, Cobb'd be ninety-six years old!

T he Oakland A's made a shambles of American League races during the early 1970s, walking off with three straight pennants. But they were not the world's most harmonious club. Conflicting personalities and their controversial owner, Charlie Finley, kept trouble brewing most of the time. Then Finley broke up the team, unloading one star after another. When asked how he felt about leaving, third baseman Sal Bando answered the question with a question. "Was it difficult leaving the *Titanic*?" he asked.

T here are football fans who will claim that playboy halfback Paul Hornung never actually broke training because he was never actually *in* training. That certainly seems to have been true during his college career at Notre Dame. Once, being caught unawares by coach Frank Leahy, Hornung quickly snuffed out a cigarette. Leahy pursued the matter. "Paul, is that a cigarette there by your feet?" he asked. "So it is, coach," said Hornung. "But you take it, you saw it first."

D uring their worst early years no one symbolized the hapless condition of the New York Mets better than first baseman Marv Throneberry. He was the good-natured butt of many of the better (and somewhat exaggerated) Mets stories. Like the time manager Casey Stengel got a cake for his birthday and someone in the clubhouse asked why Marvelous Marv hadn't got one on *his* last birthday. "We were afraid he might drop it," Stengel explained.

A mong the Great Stone Faces in professional football, you can include some of the more successful coaches: Paul Brown, Don Shula, Bud Grant, and Tom Landry. In fact, it was once rumored that Grant would automatically fine any Viking player caught smiling. A reporter familiar with both Grant and Tom Landry was once asked who he thought would win a personality contest between the two. "It would be a tie for second place," he said.

P itcher Geoff Zahn's fastball comes at you at three different speeds: slow, slower, and slowest. And because they are often effective, they generate a lot of snide comment around the league. "Some night," says Bob Lemon, "he's gonna deliver the ball and by the time it gets there, the batter will have been waived out of the league." Zahn's catcher, Bob Boone, recalls that a batter once turned and asked him if Zahn had thrown the ball yet. "Five minutes ago," said Boone. "It's just running a little late."

※

P ete Newell had just returned from coaching his University of California basketball team to the NCAA title, where his center, Darrall Imhoff, had been the tournament's sensation. Someone in the airport welcoming group mentioned that Newell's wife had broken a toe two days earlier. "Better her than Darrall Imhoff," said Newell.

O ne of the reasons that Bill Veeck got out of the baseball-owner business was the sky-rocketing salaries being paid to what he considered mediocre players. Sunning himself in the bleachers at a Cubs game, Veeck was asked if he missed owning a team. "Not at all," he said. "I can sit here and enjoy the game and when a guy drops a fly ball, I can be glad that I'm not the one paying him six hundred thousand dollars."

T he Yankee teams that dominated baseball in the late 1930s had a seemingly inexhaustible supply of talented reserves at their Newark farm club. In fact, many felt that the Newark team would finish ahead of half the clubs in the American League. Once, when outfielder Tommy Henrich was called up to the parent Yankees, Newark second baseman Joe Gordon had an explanation. "He couldn't make the team here," said Gordon.

After a pro athlete decides to retire, he almost always has second thoughts about his decision. Maybe he *should* have hung on just one more year. Pitcher Jim Colborn had that feeling—briefly—while throwing in a semipro game the year after he'd officially retired. "I was doing pretty good and started to think about making a comeback," said Colborn. "But then the second batter doubled."

Many of the newer ball parks now feature huge, TV-like screens on which instant replays can be shown. But the innovation is not universally applauded. Umpires, for example, object strenuously to the reshowing of controversial plays. Is that because they're afraid of their decisions being proved wrong? "Not at all," says one ump. "We want to avoid embarrassing fans who booed the original call."

A mong people who dislike horse racing, the thing that many of them dislike most is losing money. But other objections surface, too. The way some jockeys use their whip on their mounts, for example. Isn't that cruel and unusual punishment? Famous "whip jock" Ted Atkinson defends the practice, however. "It's simply a way to impress upon the horse the urgency of the situation," he says.

Duffy Daugherty's first love was always football. And every once in a while some diversion or other would come along to confirm his conviction that he should devote his full attention to football only. One of those occasions happened during a visit to the Santa Anita racetrack where, after a financially disastrous day, he was heard to grouse, "This is the only place I know where windows clean people."

Stanley Horn, a Nashville magazine editor, was, like most of those in his profession, a stickler for details. So he seemed annoyed when a certain congressman contended, during the late 1950s, that there was too much corruption in professional boxing. "He neglects to specify," complained Mr. Horn, "just how much corruption there *should* be."

Paul Richards was not only a superb baseball tactician, but he was also something of a diplomat. While managing the Orioles, Richards was asked to compare the rival White Sox's fine shortstop, Luis Aparicio, with the late Hall of Famer, Honus Wagner. Never one to rile the opposition, Richards declared, "Luis Aparicio is the greatest living shortstop of all time."

T he previous year had not been a good one for Mickey Mantle. And his poor statistics took their toll during the winter contract negotiations, where a disgruntled Mantle took a healthy cut in pay. Still smarting from the salary reduction when he checked in at spring training, he expressed surprise at seeing his familiar number 7 on the back of his uniform shirt. "I figured they'd cut my number to at least six and a half," he said.

※

O ur there'll-always-be-an-England entry today comes from Sir Grantley Adams, who was prime minister of the West Indies Federation back in the late 1950s. Sir Grantley was asked to comment on the unstable state of political affairs in Latin America during that period. "There would be fewer revolutions there," he sniffed, "if the people were taught to play cricket."

※

H ow do you compare athletes of different generations? Mikan versus Russell, Rose versus Cobb. Well, we don't get much help from old quarterback Sammy Baugh. Baugh was watching the Baltimore Colts on one of Johnny Unitas's better days and was asked how he would compare himself with the spectacular Johnny U. "I really don't know," said Baugh. "I never saw me play."

P ennsylvania and Ohio fans may disagree, but many football people feel that the best college prospects in the country are grown in Texas. One of the pro-Texas people was Wilbur Evans when he was the assistant athletic director at the University of Texas. Commenting on an upcoming Texas-Oklahoma game, Evans said, "We ought to be favored. We're starting eleven Texans and Oklahoma is starting only nine."

S cholarship and financial aid abuses and their resultant stiff penalties are no laughing matter today. But back in the late 1950s a lot of things were taken a bit more casually. When Michigan State's Duffy Daugherty was asked for his definition of such factors as academic achievement and need, he readily supplied both. "Academic achievement means can he read and write," said Duffy. "And need is . . . well, we don't take a boy unless we need him."

Branch Rickey's reputation as an astute trader of baseball flesh was an imposing one. He seldom came out second best in a transaction, and baseball men took to avoiding him at meetings and in hotel lobbies. Just how shrewd was the old master? Take it from Paul Richards. "Rickey's a guy who'll go into a revolving door in the section behind you," said Richards, "and come out in front of you."

✳

Frank Howard didn't have too many power-house football teams at Clemson, but one way or another he managed to win his share of games. When Clemson upset a much larger, much heavier Texas Christian team in the 1960 Blue-bonnet Bowl, Howard let us in on the secret. "Those other boys were so big they tilted the field," he said, "and we were able to play downhill all the way."

S ometimes the best thing that can happen to a youngster who aspires to be a professional athlete is to get some words of wisdom from the pros themselves. Even though the advice may be hard to follow. That was the case when a wide-eyed young lad asked Wilt Chamberlain for the key to success in basketball. "The first thing you should try to do," said Wilt, "is become seven feet tall."

✳

W hen Richie Ashburn was tearing up the National League back in the early 1960s, the word that spread among the senior circuit's pitchers was that you *had* to keep the ball low on Richie or he'd kill you. One day, with Ashburn at bat, the plate umpire asked the pitcher for a look at the ball. But when the hurler lobbed it toward the ump, Richie stepped in and drilled it to deep left center. "First pitch I've seen above the waist all year," he said.

H armon Killebrew was pounding Yankee pitching that day. In four trips to the plate he'd
homered, tripled, and had two doubles. When he
walked on his fifth at-bat, catcher Elston Howard
disagreed with the call. "*You* put him on *that*
time," said Howard to the umpire. "Maybe so,"
said the ump, "but at least I held him to one
base."

✳

F ormer Dallas Cowboy Walt Garrison does not
make any quick, impulsive judgments. When
asked whether Cowboy coach Tom Landry ever
smiles, Garrison said, "I don't know. I played
there for only nine years."

✳

I n his forties Pete Rose plays the game just as
enthusiastically as he did as a ten-year-old,
sliding headfirst in a cloud of dust, whenever the
opportunity presents itself. Have all those years
and all that money made any difference for him?
"The big difference," says Rose, "is that now my
mother doesn't have to wash the uniform."

When Gene Mauch was manager of the Minnesota Twins, he seemed equal to the potentially sensitive situation of his shortstop, Roy Smalley, being a close relative. "Sometimes I think of Roy as my nephew," said Mauch, "but sometimes only as my sister's son."

✳

Many great ballplayers turn out to be less than great managers—just as some excellent managers were only mediocre players. Rocky Bridges, who batted against Tommy Lasorda in the minors, has his own ideas on why Lasorda never made it as a pitcher. "Tommy's curve had a better hang time than a Ray Guy punt," said Bridges.

✳

As the first Joe Louis-Billy Conn fight approached, the lighter, faster Conn's strategy was obvious: He would constantly jab and retreat, using his speed and fancy footwork to try to stay out of range of Louis's heavy artillery. Would it work? Joe Louis was unconcerned. "He can run, but he can't hide," said Louis.

B ack when Jimmy Brown was terrorizing the NFL, not many defensive linemen looked forward to meeting him head on. But it was even more frightening for a defensive back to take him on after he'd broken through the line and had built up a head of steam. Take it from Charley Jackson, recalling when he was with the old Chicago Cardinals. "It's an awful sensation when Brown comes blowin' through the hole and right at you," said Jackson. "You feel like you're trapped on a trestle by an unscheduled freight train."

Branch Rickey was a notoriously shrewd judge of baseball talent and a sharp trader. His players also knew him, especially at salary negotiation time, as a man who made Scrooge look like a spendthrift. Someone once pointed out to Dizzy Dean that, since turning from the mound to broadcasting, his weight had ballooned from 160 pounds up to a pudgy 240. Was it the lack of exercise? "No," said Dean. "Back when I was playin', I was bein' paid by Mr. Rickey."

Rocky Graziano was making the perilous leap from the sweet science of boxing to the precarious world of show biz. So someone asked him if he planned to polish up his syntax with some training at a place like the famous Actors Studio. "Why should I go to a place like that?" said the Rock. "All they do is learn guys like Brando and Newman to talk like me."

P ete Rose just may be the best hitter of all time. And he may also be the game's fiercest competitor. There is general agreement, however, on one thing. With a face that resembles a clenched fist, he is not baseball's prettiest player. How does Rose explain that? "If you slid into bases head first for twenty years," he says, "you'd be ugly, too."

E veryone knows of Adolph Rupp's reputation as one of the foremost college basketball coaches of all time. But few people know that the longtime University of Kentucky round-ball genius also had a secret passion for fox hunting. Why? "Nobody loses and everybody has a good time," said Rupp. "The fox escapes, the dogs and horses get a lot of exercise, I drink some bourbon . . . and the alumni don't write letters."

W hen it came to baiting umpires, few surpassed acid-tongued manager Bill Rigney. So it came as a terrible blow to Rigney when an auto accident left him with a wired-shut broken jaw. Later he was asked if being unable to speak had taken him out of umpire hassling entirely. "Not completely," said Rigney. "I could still hiss at 'em."

M iller Barber had a problem. At fifty-one he was eligible for and enjoyed playing the Senior golf tournaments, but he was also shooting well enough to be successful on the regular PGA tour. How about going both ways then? "What you have when you play twenty Senior events and make about fifteen regular tour stops," explains Miller, "is divorce."

✳

D uring the early 1960s catcher Doug Camilli spent about two years bouncing back and forth between the Dodgers and several of their farm clubs. A week with the big team, two weeks in the minors. Ten days back up, a week back down. But how about his paycheck? Did he have a major league or a minor league contract? Apparently, that didn't matter. "The way I'd *like* to be paid," said Camilli, "is by the mile."

✳

R ichie Ashburn, one of the original Philadelphia Phillies Whiz Kids, had had a very good year and was locked in a salary dispute with the management. At one point a Phillies executive announced that the two parties weren't really very far apart. "Not much more than tip money," he said. "Maybe so," said Ashburn, "but I tip pretty good."

Before George Steinbrenner installed his unique revolving-door system of firing and rehiring Yankee managers, it was somewhat unusual for anyone in the sports world to return to a job he'd held previously. And that includes sportswriters. But Stanley Woodward returned, coming back to write his old column at the *New York Herald-Tribune* eleven years after having been fired. How do you lead off your first column after an eleven year break in the action? "As I was saying when I was so rudely interrupted . . ." Woodward began.

Index

Bengals, 16
Berra, Yogi, 35, 76, 95, 105
Berry, Raymond, 17
Blades, Ray, 71
Blair, Wren, 87
Blake, Toe, 62
Bodie, Ping, 60
Bolt, Tommy, 18
Bonds, Bobby, 51
Boone, Bob, 121
Boros, Julius, 73
Boudreau, Lou, 44, 113
Bouton, Jim, 13
Bowden, Bobby, 47
Bradshaw, Terry, 42
Bragan, Bobby, 23
Brandt, Jackie, 21
Brett, George, 48
Bridgers, John, 53
Bridges, Rocky, 131
Bristol, Dave, 80
Brock, Tom, 91
Broun, Heywood, 91
Brown, Jimmy, 132
Brown, Warren, 20
Browning, Will, 74
Browns, St. Louis, 44
Broyles, Frank, 8
Butkus, Dick, 64, 87, 90

Camilli, Doug, 135
Campbell, Earl, 28, 44
Cantillon, Joe, 101

Carnera, Primo, 91
Carter, Don, 55
Casper, Billy, 43
Castlerosse, Viscount, 82
Cedeno, Cesar, 28
Celtics, 46
Chamberlain, Wilt, 129
Chapman, Ray, 54
Cheevers, Gerry, 86
Cherry, Don, 32
Chuvalo, George, 115
Cobb, Ty, 118
Colborn, Jim, 123
Conley, Gene, 32
Conn, Billy, 131
Connors, Chuck, 108
Cooke, Jack Kent, 96
Cosell, Howard, 117
Cousy, Bob, 12
Cowens, Dave, 46
Cruz, Jose, 50
Cubs, 20

Dangerfield, Rodney, 65
Dantley, Adrian, 30
Daugherty, Duffy, 32, 66,
    117, 125, 127
Davis, Glenn, 109
Dawkins, Darrell, 72
Dean, Dizzy, 41, 42, 103,
    104, 133
Demaret, Jimmy, 19, 24, 99
Denson, Al, 84